1980

PAUSES

SALLY LOVE SAUNDERS

PAUSES

THE GOLDEN QUILL PRESS
Publishers

Francestown   New Hampshire

Library of Congress Catalog Card Number 78-51847

ISBN 0-8233-0272-5

First printing May 1978
Second printing October 1978

Printed in the United States of America

DEDICATION

To Miriam — my teacher and dear friend

CONTENTS
(Titles and First Lines)

PAUSES

A POEM

A poem is an unexpected house guest
Who arrives with a suitcase.
Immediately, he unpacks
And settles down.

A poem is an unexpected house guest
Who recalls old experiences,
Suddenly giving them new light.

Yes, a poem is a house guest,
For after he has gone
It seems as though he is still there.

13

WORDS WANT TO BE CALLED ON

Words want to be called on
to be lined up to speak
they're waiting
calling out
frustrated
restless.
I, their leader,
stand helpless
because I can not
remember their names
not even one.

IT PUSHES THROUGH

A poem stars as a gurgling
a rumbling — a gasping for air.
It pushes through to sunlight
oxygen and room.

CHILD OF THE CAPE

Oh, sea gull
You were constructed
From that where you live.
Focussed out of the gray and white air,
Your creviced mouth
Is a part of a rock.
Your feet,
Merely cold twigs
From one of last winter's branches.
When you sit,
You resemble a block of driftwood.
Reflecting the waves you do
In sight and motion.
You are entitled then to fly past the sun
To read THE message printed there!
And when you die,
You'll glide with the mist;
Thus melting into the Cape
From whence you came.

MINDS

A refined mind is
a shaved branch;
A child's mind is
covered with blooms
and feathers.

OUR DECISION

We sat on the sand
Facing each other
For we wanted to construct a castle.
He poured on sand — and
I poured on sand
Until we had built our decision.

My heart
an Indian's drum
beating out the message
of your name.

Full crystal dandelions
are like stars
And when they blow
galaxies
and the universe.

MELANCHOLY

Melancholy,
walking
down the corridor
of my mind,
scuffs and kicks
odd stones.

THE MOON

The moon is a silent guest
Who stands alone,
Watches
And glows.
The moon grows
Fast like a child
Until full grown
And wrinkled,
It passes on.

Sea gulls —
carefully trained
and practiced
Ballet dancers in the sky.

WALKING ALONG THE SHORE

As I walk,
As though on blotter paper
Thick and porous
I enjoy soaking into
And watching
My weight count.
Engrossed, I watch
The ocean gather into itself
And lunge
As a wild cat does
With his fur flying.

HUSBAND

Husband, you're my other book end —
not fastened but mated.
We hold between us
travel books, poems of rhyme
and letters unanswered
that probably never will be answered.
Sometimes our books fall
and sometimes they stand tall.
Husband, I'm talking to you
way over there.

Sweetheart,
I love it when
we're relaxed
and our hearts melt together
like two pats of butter
running into a Liquid Pool
of Yellow.

I love you so much
my heart is as big
as a beach ball.

ON MARRIAGE

Sometimes the gap is so wide
I think in terms of
The Grand Canyon
where the deep,
bottomless distances
are wide from side to side.
Sometimes we are of one skin
and one frame.
My blood runs in your veins
and your blood runs in mine.
The tide comes in
and the tide goes out.
Yes, the pulse of life
is both low and high.

A ROSE PETAL

I'd like to slide down a rose petal
On my back
And crouch on the bottom
And then look up.
I'd like to wrap the petal
All around me
Until I am asleep.

COMMUNICATION

Two rows of single flash lights
Their rays crossing.
Two rows of flash lights
Their rays meeting
And blending into single rays.

INDIAN SUMMER

A soft Breeze echoes
The days to dream,
The days to get softened.

Oh! What a long thought it takes
To think of winter,
Of all those hours of cold ahead.

Home is summer —
But time is pulling it away
Those raindrops are turning to ice.

SPRING IN NEW ENGLAND

Spring is restrained in New England;
It isn't a symphony played by a full orchestra
But a well-disciplined concerto.
In New England, Spring stands erect
Inside a tulip.
The breezes do not make me ecstatic;
Instead, they make me smile.
They are not everlasting fields
Through which I want to fly.
But plots of land surrounded by stone walls
Enclosing miniature beauty
As on Japanese fans.

THERE'S A MOSQUITO OF WORRY

There's a mosquito of worry
Buzzing, buzzing around my head.
I swat it to leave but it won't.
Nothing but its drone is heard —
the room filled with its noise.
Wish I could run out
and leave it behind
but it clings and follows me
all over the place —
Buzzing louder and louder.

THE WIND

The wind is a
growling old grouch
who wants to be let in.

FRUSTRATION

Frustration
claws and paces
back and forth
inside me.
Its mane and tail
sail behind
in the wind.

NON INVOLVEMENT

She goes to the zoo
looks at the animals
but does not feed them.
She goes to the art museum
sees the statues
but doesn't feel them.
She went to the beach
but never allowed
the salt to sting her.
She shook his hand
but never held it.

THE FOG

The fog all night long
turns somersaults
in the bay.
When the dim day breaks,
it subtly suggests
there are boats
in the harbour.

Hurting — healing
Mending is a time
I must withdraw
and mend
the broken down
pieces of my insides.
A time of mending
quiet
do not disturb.
People scare and hurt
me now
except for one
who reminds me of my dog.
I'm scared of highways
and airplanes
and people's problems.
I need to knit quietly
the frayed pieces of my insides
I need my physical surroundings
to be neat
because pain is not neat.
I cannot give now
for I am dry
I have no fuel
just hurt and pain
and the need to not be seen.
I am like an old gray haired lady
in front of a fireplace knitting her insides
together.

The tide has left
leaving seaweed;
memories
on the shore.
The tide has forgotten
about the seaweed —
it's off
pounding on another shore.

You know last night a prince came.
And there have been other princes in my life.
As a little girl I was taught
there would be One prince
and He would come
and carry me off on His horse.
But, now I'm a big girl
and I realize there are many princes.
Some rides long — some short
many royal balls
and many times to stand on my toes.
The trick is to get off their horse (Volkswagen)
before they turn into a frog
and I'm left sitting in the mud.

The early morning sun
washes the city of
yesterday's hurts.

I enjoy riding the bus
as it purrs along.
I feel like I'm riding in the belly
of a cat.

It's nice to be home
to sort the papers from the weekend
into the circulatory system of my home
To get some perspective
to feel big again.
The drive was delicious
the unwinding felt right
It was part of the whole experience.
It's a relief to be away
from all the sensory bombardments
and flying glistening comets
It was Christmas shopping
with all the lights
music
excitement.
Home is a refuge and it's quiet
and settled.

I have a friend who keeps his feelings
neatly piled in a brief case
that's unscuffed.
Once in a while a bit of one
will leak out of the side
but he quickly tucks it back in.

The days so stuffed
with things to do
going from point A
to point B
stretching to get there on time
carrying this
carrying that
answering to this
then he walks up
and says to my army
go the other way
The soldiers drop their guns
and want to quit.
So, it's nice to just be here
for a minute
not running here
not running there
But the noise of what I must do
makes this moment ever more precious.

Whirling — spinning
Friday shoppers twirled me like a top
with the string tight
Even the hands of the clock
squeezed me today
I'm afraid you got some
of my sparks spinning off
for awhile
But now the spinning has stopped
and I'm very much settled into
being quiet with you.

Carnivals demanding
eat here
ride this
red blink
throw toss
excitement
more excitement
my adrenalin
greets and meets
pulsating
beating
I love it all.
But — you know
later I'm left robbed
of my body's fuel
depleted
empty.

Jimmy tickles me gently
and slowly
I lie still
moving a little
like a cat in the sun —
the nice pain of too much tenderness
whispers through my body
and afterwards
I'm left wonderfully full.

You took my heart
to the top
of the Empire State Building
and dropped it.
It broke on the cement
into a million pieces.

I'm leaving you Jimmy —
pulling away from your wooden dock
with its splinters
to journey out into the ocean.
Now you can feel my motion of leaving
and can see me still in detail
but gradually I'll disappear.
Maybe I'll write you a message
and put it in a bottle to be delivered
to you.
It hurt too much being tied up
to your dock —
the lines were so tight
I rubbed and got bruised.
I need to focus on the sky
and the water now —
good bye.

I'm calm now
my hurricane has blown over
and I can see the damage
of too much force.
Walking along, I'm sorry
for the damage.
I hope you can remember when
this wind was at times
a gentle breeze
that caressed you.

In confusion and chaos,
I grab onto a buoy of insights
rest on an island of theory
sun myself in your love.
Sometimes I feel like a cocktail shaker inside
It's so peaceful when
we drink hot cider
with the cinnamon sticks you gave me
and the phone is asleep
and the world seems to be still too.
Even the cat isn't meowing.

More is said in gentleness
than when anger tries to patch
a hole in us.
I don't mean to cause holes.
I feel as a potter wanting
to smooth and caress the clay bowl.

You are cozy and love me
like my fireplace
when the fire is crackling
your beard the logs —

Wanting to get into quiet places
lanes
as the fat car plows on
licking up the white road lines
with the car on automatic
city lights swallowed in its insides.

I'm remembering seagulls glide up
on wind currents
and that's what I want
to find quiet spaces
and glide.

I don't want to talk
to relate with energy flowing
don't even want to be excited
or turned on

I just want to be with you
quiet
uninspired
no stars popping out of me
just be calm
just be
just be

The day will move like a fast current
I'll have to struggle to stay afloat
so now I'm here
soon I'll be on the road
cars passing
me passing cars
so I'd like to grab
a few minutes of quiet.
The clock is eating away at our peace
but while there is a little left
I want to keep it.

I want to talk with you in silences
maybe a sigh
for hour after hour
mile after mile
unfolding
trees passing
monotonous tones of car
rolling along the highway.
I have spun on my toes
round and round
now I want to be still.
The black night like cotton
cushioning us a jewel in a box.

Words protect me from saying
what I really want to say.

It's nice to vacate
cut the line
that holds you to the shore
To do nothing
Oh, how nice to do nothing
to waste time
to splash minutes around
lavishly
To do nothing is so refreshing.

Quiet — so healing
like bubbling water
that takes the kinks away
and purifies them over the rocks
they drop out of the stream
forming sand
that too becomes lovely
Quiet flows
in its colorless rhythm

Bathing in quiet
soaking in its rays
massages my being
and strokes —

I'm floating on the lake
of solitude
cool
smooth waters.
The water mattresses me
ripples coming toward me.
Time doesn't tick here.
The air hums.

You said you hadn't unpacked
I am glad
for I too have not unpacked
the feelings
the glows.
The sunsets have not been
tucked away
into the horizon's shelf.

I love my dog
because she doesn't
have to do anything.
She just is.
She doesn't take on
a lot of projects.
She refuses to contaminate
herself in the polluted stream
of nonsense.
She is simply herself.
Her joy is greeting me and
going for walks.
She doesn't concern herself
about tomorrow.
She is
and that is enough.

OH, WE LIVE AS PIECES OF A PUZZLE

Oh, we live as pieces of a puzzle
fitted together tentatively
to be jumbled up anytime
be anyone.
We then lay scattered
separated and turned around.
We are disjointed
turned around and upside down.
Tomorrow maybe some hand
will settle us again.

NO PAIN IS SHARPER

No pain is sharper
and cuts into me
deeper
than the pain caused
by watching the petals
fall off one I love.
I can stand the outside layers
falling
but when it gets to peeling
the inner core,
that is wretched.
Death disregards a rose's modesty
and lays it opened and exposed.
Before the old I love die,
they are with me
but something is pulling
them away.
She will leave
even though I cry
and don't want her to leave.
Should I give her my tears
as a parting gift of love?

A DISAPPOINTMENT

When a disappointment comes,
It whistles
For its cousins and friends
Who've just been waiting.
In they run —
Wearing cleats — to do their dance.

THIS CANDLE

A candle that is only
a little alive
crippled, reaching,
Hurts and longs for extinction.

"Wind, wind, put me out.
This shivering and crouching
Hurts.
Save me from my misery
Put me out."

HEALTH

Health, I want you
to wear your bright suit
to walk with light feet
and be on my toes.
Health, I wish to be full
of your juice of life.
I wish to own
and carry you in my arms.

A MOUNTAIN

To be a mountain,
You'd have to sit on a steady pole
That makes you stiff.
In fog,
Toward the sky you'd stand on tiptoes.
Bow to climbers
Twist for skiers,
And open your arms
So they could slide away.

TO DUKE ELLINGTON *

I know what you mean
And are saying —
Those times so few
That are felt so fully.
I know so well
That it is too personal to clap —
Don't ask me to.
I am too full with feeling
To jump around.
I am stunned and paralyzed —
Clapping would be vulgar
And not right.

* Written while listening to Duke Ellington at
St. John Terrell's Music Circus July 19, 1965

YOU AND THE SYMPHONY *

You and the symphony are in rapport
And so you can love out of understanding.
You can slide together
In your own way
And feel brittlely.
Your sensitivity walks lightly.
When you pound,
You mean it.
With trumpets, you rejoice.
It is in here
You can live and belong.
Stamp, leap,
Bounce with your joy!

* Written while listening to Van Cliburn play Rachmaninoff's
Piano Concerto No. 3 at the Robin Hood Dell — July 29, 1965

AMAL JAMAL

The keys come to you
For you —
With you, too, they come alive
And live not flat.
The piano longs for you
As you do for it.
Amal Jamal — an artist —
For you and your medium are one.
Here is your being,
Your center of existence.
The paint falls off the piano
And the sap returns as you.
Tap out the beat of life.
Claw for and cling to
Your keys so fine.
Grab them and hold them firm —
Cling madly
For they are your salvation —
You sing of and with the great themes —
Those immortal themes —
And yet,
You play the most basic beat
Of all the men that have ever been.
The crowd is unaware —
How much so, I don't know —
The immortal theme
And man's beat are one!
Hallelujah!
So simple and easy by you.

THE GRAND CANYON

Nature is generous.
It spreads its beautiful makings
Lavishly
As does the chef at an abundant banquet.
Here the sun gets shattered.
Time and motion stand silently
Absorbing the pulse of the days.
A star falls
As does a tear roll,
Shed because of too much beauty.

AFRICA

Africa is a symphony
Of earth, animals and people
Undivided;
The symphony plays loud
And mighty with unmatched gusto.
The people wear the earth
And the earth lives with them;
Their homes are earth and man,
And always have been.
I sing to you of Africa
With full lungs and a full voice.
Mountain blends into mountain,
Generation into generation.
There are no stop watches
And traffic lights to try to beat;
Time and space have no boundaries.
They stretch on and wide
As does the native's patience.
I sing to you of Africa
With full lungs and a full voice.
It's a vigorous land
With strong healthy colors;
Wheat fields vibrating
With silver stalks.
Africa is the land of life;
Natives working hard with the earth.
It's a tender land —
Long banana trees flapping with the winds,
Tiny flowers with flawless petals.

Africa is a symphony
Of earth, animals and people
Undivided.

REDWOODS

Redwoods, there was that time
That hungry fire ate at your insides
Leaving you hollow and empty.
But you grew
Slowly and patiently
From that in you which was still alive.
Till now you are gallant and admirable.
You give me strength and solace
As I make my pilgrimage to your feet
And bow with respect.
Yes, I, seeing the burnt-out area
That is still a part of you,
Know and understand
There was that time
That hungry fire ate at your insides
Leaving you hollow and empty.

MAILED MY GUTS

My guts were dropped
down into a mail chute.
They fell and fell
and seem to be
falling still.

My guts incased
in white sheets
sent out into the wind.
What will come back?
I hope not
emptiness in my mailbox.

IF I COULD BUT LEAVE BEHIND ME

If I could but leave behind me
a wall of words
neatly stacked
with end fitting into end —
Bringing a sense of order
to the disgruntled motorist.

LOVE

Love is a fan
That can open quickly or slowly —
To flutter — to sway
Or to close again.

LOVE THOUGHTS

When we're apart
I'm a half of a grapefruit
wizzened — dried up.
With you I'm a full plump
whole
yellow grapefruit.

Drinking glass with the confines of skin
tight holding confining
while bubbles inside
rush to the top
to air to express
So my words are
my bubbles from within
So carbonated with you
so fresh
the pop from the bottle
still in the air.

We're two balloons floating —
up and away
our strings entwined.
So much helium in the balloon —
the sun reflecting on them.

You are definitely with me
wherever I go.
I carry you in a papoose
on my heart.

I'm on the tippy end
of a kite string
flapping and floating
and gliding
The breezes tickling me gently.

I've been on the ground
too long
I miss your updraft
that used to pick me up
and carry me off
on wings of silver.

You a dancer
me a dancer
not able to follow.
Two solo dancers
can dance together
and energize.
The wind from their freedom
Their lack of fear from being free
Giving joy to the other.
Whee! look at us —
so free!
The individual strength that each has
joining them together.

TO MARK

Walking in the autumn woods
stretching over logs
creeping under fallen trees
with a stream that sometimes
follows us.
We came to a spot
to sit — to be comfortable
to rest for awhile.
And so with our love
we've struggled with logs
in our path
and now have come to a spot
where we can enjoy
and rest.

Such a celebration of life
this fall —
confetti leaves still clinging
    to the stream
Today we turned our clocks back
the party is ending.
My love and I will find
a winter festival of beauty.

It's 4:30 a.m. the rain and wind are
                    crackling outside
wrapping me and insulating me
tucking me in over and over.
I wish you were here
and we could just listen to the rain and wind
together.
We fit together so perfectly you and I
The rain and wind are looking for you
                    all over.
There's a bittersweet quality of being apart
    from you
this time
A relief to find again that neutral place
in me alone once more
and yet a longing to share the music of the rain
                    and wind with you here in bed.

We are two identical stars
apart — pinned to separate spots
but giving forth the same
light and glow
Twin stars close together
off in our own space in the galaxy
away from the busy milky way
and changing neon signs,
Together yet apart
The same glow uniting us
connected also by our own special light.

Remember those two stars
that were me and my love
last night?
Well, tonight there is only one star there.
A fat — stuffed shining star.
It looks as though it ate
the other star.
The other star gone
devoured into the big star
not a trace left of me.
Yikes!

Your love tide
is in
High tide
Flooding my shores
The sun glistening on the water.
Full tide
Swollen with love.

Then . . .
there are times
the tide of your love
Pulls out
away from me
Leaving the shore parched
dry
empty
No water in sight.
I can't reach the water.
Maybe a single wave
will splash in
and then leave.

But now the tide is in
erasing the marks of low tide.

Perhaps there's a rhythm
I need to learn
and accept
and feel comfortable with.
The tides of your love
are like the tides of the ocean.

You know how a sock feels
when it's inside out —
all rough and edgy?
Well, that's how
I've been feeling
But now you've turned the sock
right side around.
I'm smooth again.

I'm caught on your hook
wriggling
squirming
Your delicious bait enticed me.
Now I'm caught
no matter how hard I wiggle
the hook won't let go.
You're pulling me to the dock
where you'll skin
and cut me up in pieces.

I was just a game
of tetherball.
When I'd come in close,
You would swat me hard
to send me off.
Then wait with your paddle
until I'd return
then wham!
off you'd send me again.

Well, I've taken myself
off the line
I'm not a game for you
now.
The pole does not have me
on it.
I've been bashed enough.
I'm not going to be
your tetherball any longer.

Because you love me
you hate me too at times.
The love I enjoy
but when the thin coin is flipped over,
and you talk to me from that side,
it is hard.
One side of all coins is a face
with eyes, skin — a person — feelings
The other side inanimate objects
or an eagle with claws that can kill.
When you're flipped onto your hate side
it's your horizon then —
no traces of the human side.
And so with the other side,
To be loved by you
brings both love and hate to me.

It used to be
the waves of your love
would rush to me
when I'd come on the beach
they would cover me all up
with their foam
licking my face.
Now I start to come to the beach
and you are far out in the sea
you may move a little
in my direction
but then choose not to roll
to me.
You'd rather play with a buoy
or remain still watching the sky.

And so I sit lonely and abandoned
and for solace pour sand over my toes.
But I miss the way
the waves of your wanting were
and the beach seems empty
without them.
I can see you out there
but you're not rushing to me
anymore.

It doesn't matter to Mark
if my feelings fall to the floor
like spill from a saw
sawing wood —
the saw tearing through the wood
moving how It wants —
"The sawdusts' feelings
are light and can be swept away,"
thinks the saw.

Your hostility swatted me dead
today
A flattened out fly
no more buzzing
flying
walking on my legs.
I'm dead now
flat
motionless.
You seem to like me dead.

You've left me —
back into your coiled shell
empty space between us —
I reach into the shell
but am met with cold drops of water
The emptiness is so big and dark
    and ominous.
. . . a bubble from your breathing
but —

We have come apart
will we meet and discover each other again
or will we grow
farther apart?
The space between us
is like a canal in the Arctic
with very cold water in it.
We're two icebergs.
I can't stand the cold.

We didn't break up
we tore apart
like molasses being pulled
painfully
slowly
then wadded back together
for more to be pulled from.
The stretching going out
so-o   v-e-r-y   t-h-i-n.

Why do I stand here
cold
unfed
alone
with all this space in front of me?
Why?
I hate myself for not leaving —
Oh I go aside a little
but never leave.
Will I just become finally
eaten and devoured
until the destroyer
wipes me out too.

My weariness and weakness
prevent me from leaving.
And I love this area
even though
it's only a shell now.
I'm loving the remains
of what was.
Content to stay with the echo
more than look for new meadows.
I guess there's hope in me
that the wind will return
the green.

Two balloon strings
Released
from a clenched fist —
floating upward
the sun hugging their sides.
Their strings
like lazy fingers
draped overboard from a rowboat
into the very refreshing water.
Different winds carrying them
in different directions.

It's nice, you know,
to be alone and alive
to swing on mental high bars
far and wide.
Giving is good
but thinking alone
is good too.

So don't knock at me
to share.
I'm tired of reaching out
and want to lie still.

Space in front of me
where what used to be
soft and green grass
flowers butterflies and
humming bees
Fierce winds ate up
the thick grass
the flowers
and the butterflies
My ground taken away
in front of me.
Now I'm standing on a cliff
space which was once ground
is in front of me.
Winds howling trying to
throw me off.
Occasionally, a tumbleweed
blows past.
But doesn't rest
doesn't last.
And so our relationship
was once solid
and growing
has been eaten up and destroyed
by your destructiveness.
I've hung on with less and less
ground under me
Now only a cliff
The tumbleweeds your promises
that float by
not meaning to stay.

I'm bubbling
like I'm a glass of Alka Seltzer
You've dropped a tablet
down my head
and I'm percolating with love.

I read over my book of poems
about our love
and I was able to see
that we've been on the rocks
throughout.
Then I realized
you need for us to be on the rocks
so your beach will be clear of me.
You allow the waves of my passion
to come in briefly
but then you push it to the rocks.
So, our love has been on the rocks —
the rocks its home.

Your kisses
sound like raindrops
falling on the window pane.

POETIC ELECTRICITY

Beauty generates poetic electricity
Which has run through the air
Even before life began.
Poets have tried to harness it
And have gotten a little
Into poems to suit their souls
To suit the times
Yet always leaving
This poetic electricity uncaptured.